PUBLICATIONS OF THE AMERICAN INSTITUTE OF MUSICOLOGY

ARMEN CARAPETYAN, Ph. D.
DIRECTOR

CORPVS SCRIPTORVM DE MVSICA

5

ANONYMOUS

NOTITIA DEL VALORE DELLE NOTE DEL CANTO MISURATO

(A 14th-Century Treatise in the Vulgate)

AMERICAN INSTITUTE OF MUSICOLOGY

CORPVS SCRIPTORVM DE MVSICA

5

ANONIMI

NOTITIA DEL VALORE DELLE NOTE DEL CANTO MISVRATO

EDIDIT

ARMEN CARAPETYAN

1957

AMERICAN INSTITUTE OF MUSICOLOGY

Printed in Holland by "Centrale Drukkerij" Nijmegen

CONTENTS

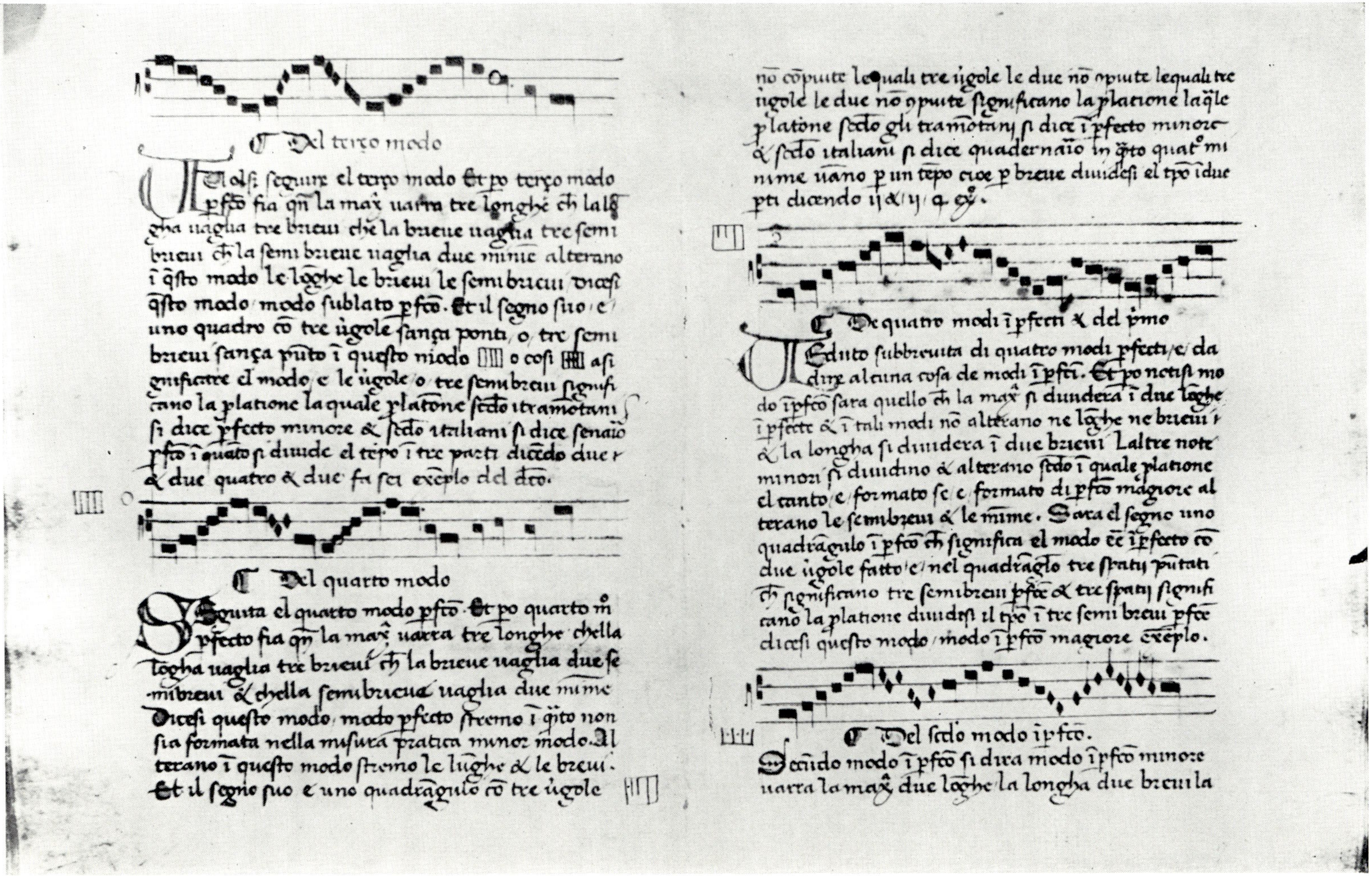

Del terço modo

Volsi seguire el terço modo. Et po terço modo
pfto sia qn la max narra tre longhe ch la lõg
gha naglia tre brevi che la breve naglia tre semi
brevi ch la semibreve naglia due minie alterano
i qsto modo le loghe le brevi le semibrevi dicesi
qsto modo modo sublato pfto. Et il segno suo e
uno quadro cō tre ugole sança ponti, o tre semi
brevi sança puto i questo modo o cosi a si
gnificare el modo e le ugole o tre semibrevi signifi
cano la platione la quale platone scdo itramotani
si dice pfecto minore & scdo italiani si dice senario
pfto i quato si divide el tepo i tre parti dicedo due e
& due quatro & due fa sei exeplo del dto.

Del quarto modo

Seguita el quarto modo pfto. Et po quarto m
pfecto sia qn la max narra tre longhe chella
logha naglia tre brevi ch la breve naglia due se
mibrevi & chella semibreve naglia due mime
Dicesi questo modo modo pfecto stremo i qsto non
sia formata nella misura pratica minor modo. Al
terano i questo modo stremo le lunghe & le brevi.
Et il segno suo e uno quadragulo cō tre ugole

nō cōputte le quali tre ugole le due nō oputte le quali tre
ugole le due nō oputte significano la platione la qle
platone scdo gli tramotani si dice i pfecto minore
& scdo italiani si dice quadernaio in qsto quat° mi
nime nano p un tepo cioe p breve dividesi el tpo i due
pti dicendo ii & ii, 4 &c.

De quatro modi i pfecti & del pmo

Veduto subbrevita di quatro modi pfecti, e da
dire alcuna cosa de modi i pfti. Et po notisi mo
do i pfto sara quello ch la max si dividera i due loghe
i pfecte & i tali modi nō alterano ne loghe ne brevi i
& la longha si dividera i due brevi. Laltre note
minori si dividino & alterano scdo i quale platione
el canto e formato se e formato di pfto magiore al
terano le semibrevi & le mime. Sara el segno uno
quadragulo i pfto ch significa el modo ee i pfecto co
due ugole fatte e nel quadraglo tre spatij putati
ch significano tre semibrevi pfte & tre spatij signifi
cano la platione dividesi il tpo i tre semi brevi pfte
dicesi questo modo modo i pfto magiore exeplo.

Del scdo modo i pfto.

Secondo modo i pfto si dira modo i pfto minore
narra la max due loghe la longha due brevi la

Fol. 16v — 17r

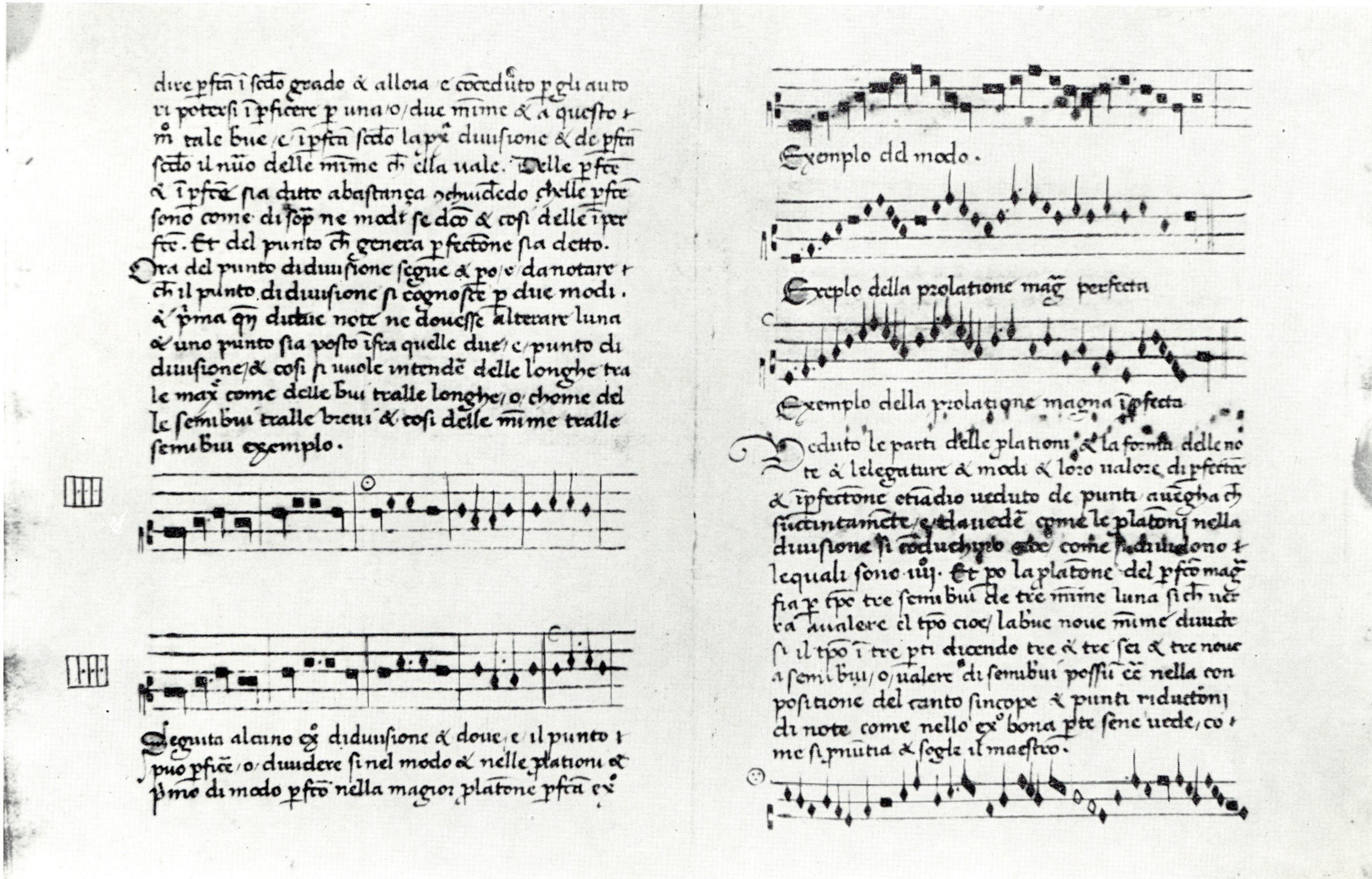

dire p̄fta i scdo grado & allora e concedūto p gli auto
ri potersi i p̄ficere p una o due mime & a questo t
m̄ tale bue e ipfta scdo la p̄a diuisione & de pfta
scdo il nūo delle mime ch ella uale. Delle pfte
& i pfte sia dutto abastança schiudēdo chelle pfte
sono come di sop ne modi se dco & cosi delle ipfe
fte. Et del punto ch genera pfectione sia detto.
Ora del punto di diuisione segue & po e da notare t
ch il punto di diuisione si cognosce p due modi.
& pma qn dirtue note ne douesse alterare luna
& uno punto sia posto ifra quelle due e punto di
diuisione & cosi si uuole intendē delle longhe tra
le max come delle bui tralle longhe o chome del
le semibui tralle breui & cosi delle mime tralle
semibui exemplo.

Seguita alcuno ex di diuisione & doue e il punto t
puo pfice o diuidere si nel modo & nelle plationi &
pmo di modo pfto nella magior platone pfta ex

Exemplo del modo.

Exeplo della prolatione mag perfecta

Exemplo della prolatione magna ipfecta

Veduto le parti delle plationi & la forma delle no
te & le legature & modi & loro ualore di pfectio
& ipfectione etiadio ueduto de punti auegha ch
succintamente [illegible] come le platonj nella
diuisione si conduchino [illegible] come si diuidono t
lequali sono iiij. Et po la platone del pfto mag
sia p tpo tre semibui de tre mime luna si ch uer
ra a ualere el tpo cioe la bue noue mime diuide
si il tpo i tre pti dicendo tre & tre sei & tre noue
a semibui o ualere di semibui possu ce nella con
positione del canto sincope & punti riductionj
di note come nello ex bona pte sene uede co t
me si pnutia & sogle il maestro.

Fol. 19v — 20r

FOREWORD*

Music history is perhaps coming to recognize a Florentine school of the pre-Medici period, though unable as yet to trace origins and early development. Whether or not the term "school" may appropriately be applied, we know by now an outstanding group formed of such talented composers as Francesco, Giovanni, Gherardello, Jacopo (da Firenze), Lorenzo Masini, Piero, Donato da Cascia, all active during the 14th century, as also men as Paolo (at the turn of the century) and Andrea dei Servi (active early in the 15th century).

These musicians carried polyphonic art to one of its summits. Francesco (Landini) has already been compared with the great French master Guillaume de Machaut; the others will be better known as their works are brought to light (in *Corpus Mensurabilis Musicae*).

We may safely assume that thanks to such men Florence of the 14th century was a brilliant centre of music. And we are fortunate enough to be heirs to charming masterpieces of a lyrical kind from that epoch. This heritage surely implies the existence of a polyphonic art grown out of a rich soil of local tradition, and which, besides producing the works of the Florentines themselves, later influenced the works of a Guillaume Dufay.

Such a rich tradition had doubtless also its theoretical

* An article on the present treatise, containing some of the introductory material here given, appeared in *Musica Disciplina* IV, 1950.

spokesmen. But history has left us no treatise that might be considered as the particular theoretical expression of the Florentine art. To be sure, Italy of the 14th century does not abound with theoretical works, and her most important theorist of the time, Marchettus of Padua, was separated from the banks of the Arno not only by distance but by differing political and social conditions.

The treatise here presented is one of the three theoretical works of probably Florentine origin so far come down to us, and it undoubtedly represents an oral tradition of musical teaching in Florence of the 14th century [1]. It cannot be considered as the formulation of the doctrine that nourished the works of the great Florentine masters, for its teaching is rather elementary. Nevertheless, it may be classed with the important treatises of polyphony of the age because of its abundant and original terminology, and because it is one of the very few instances of a treatise written in the Tuscan dialect and of popularization of musical theory. Moreover, it helps us to reconstruct the spirit as well as curriculum of mensuralist instruction in 14th-century Florence.

Florence, Spring 1951.

[1] Of the other two, the rather inconsequential *Arte del biscanto misurato secondo il maestro Iacopo da Bologna* (found in the same codex containing our treatise) was published by J. Wolf in *Theodore Kroyer, Festschrift zum sechzigsten Geburtstage . . .*, Regensburg, 1933. The third equally uninteresting treatise of Florentine origin, *Ars ad adiscendum contrapunctum secundum Magistrum Paulum de Florentia*, is found in the manuscript Ashburnham 1119 at the Bibl. Mediceo-Laurenziana.

MANUSCRIPTS CITED

Siglum	
BL	Bologna, Liceo musicale, Q 15 (37) — 15th century — music.
Ch	Chantilly, Musée Condé, ms. 1047 — 15th century — music.
Ashb B	Florence, Bibl. Laurenziana, Ashburnham 1119 — 15th century — treatises.
Pal	Florence, Bibl. Laurenziana, Palatina 87 — 15th century — music.
Re	Florence, Bibl. Laurenziana, Redi 71 — 15th century — treatises.
Iv	Ivrea, Bibl. capitolare, ms. without shelf-number — 14th century — music.
7369	Paris, Bibl. nat., lat. 7369 — 15th century — treatises.
15128	Paris, Bibl. nat., lat. 15128 — 14th century — treatises.
P	Paris, Bibl. nat., ital. 568 — 15th century — music.
Pi	Pisa, Bibl. univ., ms. 606 — 15th century — treatises.
Mur Pal	Rome, Bibl. Vat., Pal. lat. 1377 — 15th century — treatises.
Str	Strasbourg, Bibl. nat., M. 222 C. 22 — 15th century — treatises and music. Ms destroyed in 1870.
Trém	Château de Serrant (Maine), France, double leaf of a lost 14th century Ms containing music.

WORKS CITED

Besseler, Heinrich, "Studien zur Musik des Mittelalters" in *Archiv für Musikwissenschaft* 7 (1925-1926), 167-252; 8 (1926-1927), 137-258.

Coussemaker, Edmond de, *Scriptorum de musica medii aevi* . . ., Paris, 1864-1876. 4 vols.

Sartori, Claudio, *La Notazione italiana del trecento in una redazione inedita del "Tractatus practice cantus mensurabilis ad modum Ytalicorum" di Prosdocimo de Beldemandis*. Firenze, 1938.

Theodor Kroyer- Festschrift zum sechzigsten Geburtstage am 9. September 1933 . . ., Regensburg, 1933.

Van den Borren, Charles, *Le Manuscrit musical M. 222 C. 22 de la Bibliothèque de Strasbourg (XVe siècle) brulé en 1870, et reconstitué d'après une copie partielle d'Edmond de Coussemaker*, Anvers, 1924.

Wolf, Johannes, *Geschichte der Mensural-Notation von 1250-1460* . . ., Leipzig, 1904. 3 vols.

ABBREVIATIONS USED IN THE PRESENT VOLUME

Certain abbreviations generally used and understood have not been included in the following list. It is understood that Latin abbreviations stand for all forms of nouns, verbs and adjectives, unless otherwise indicated.

AfM	*Archiv für Musikwissenschaft*
AN	*Ars nova* (treatise)
br.	*brevis*
cod.	*codex*
CS	Coussemaker, *Scriptores*
def.	*deficit*
Ex.	Example — *exemplum*
fig.	*figura*
LCM	*Libellus cantus mensurabilis*
lig.	*ligatura*
lo.	*longa*
marg.	*margo*
max.	*maxima*
min.	*minima*
om.	*omisit*
pa.	*pausa*
pu. div.	*punctus divisionis*
pu. perf.	*punctus perfectionis*
sb.	*semibrevis*
semimin.	*semiminima*
seq.	*sequitur*
T.	*Tenor*
WGM	Wolf, *Geschichte der Mensural-Notation*

THE CODEX

The present treatise is contained in but a single source, the manuscript Redi 71 (**Re**) of the Biblioteca Mediceo-Laurenziana at Florence. The codex is a small volume, measuring 216 x 144 mm., whose original brown leather binding, somewhat restored, has been conserved. A later hand has inscribed on the back of this binding: "Regole del canto". There are 81 paper folios, plus 2 parchment fly-leaves; the recto of the first of these, and ff. 60-81 are blank. The folios have been numbered by a modern hand with Arabic numerals.

The manuscript was copied in the first years of the 15th century by a very legible hand, who used with moderation the ordinary abbreviations of the period. The initials and the titles are in red; the volume is otherwise devoid of any kind of ornamentation. While the pages bear marks of long use, the manuscript is still in good condition, and apparently intact. An *ex-libris* on the verso of the first fly-leaf reads: "A uso di s̄r landomina". On ff. 18v, 19r, 25r, 25v, 26v, 27r, 27v, 28r, 28v, red notes are included in the musical examples.

The following is an inventory of the whole contents of the manuscript, which contains seven musical treatises, all in the Tuscan dialect:

INCIPIT AND EXPLICIT

Ff.

1r „Tavola"

1. 2r „Ad avere alcuna noticia del canto & prima della mano.

Per che nota la mano avere xx positioni"

13r „. . . succinctamente allo scolaro per canto piano. Deo gratias Amen"

2. 13r „Per avere alcuna notitia del valore delle note del canto misurato et di loro divisione
Per che dico essere note del canto misurato sei"

24r „. . . piu volte repetuta parebbe et non altro. Deo gratias"

3. 24v „Ad avere alcuna notitia del contrapunto
Per che dico il contrapunto richiede avere"

28v „. . . ut al la per grado in viiia. Exemplo" (follows a vacant stave).

4. 29r „Ciascuno che desidera essere amaestrato assai competentemente nell' arte pratica del misurabil canto servi quelle cose diligentemente le quali seguitano somariamente secundo il maestro giovani de çuri.
Cinque sono le parti della prolatione"

40v „. . . et cosi si fanno diverse note" (examples follow on fol. 41r — This is a translation of the *LCM* attributed to Johannes de Muris).

5. 41v „Questa é l'arte del biscanto misurato secundo el maestro iacopo da bologna
Queste sono regole et divisioni dell' arte musica"

48v „. . . vaglono tre minime cosi come qui (Example) Deo gratias. Amen" [2].

6. 48v „Dico che noi abbiamo nel contrapuncto quattro gradi"

59r „. . . ordine che é prestitivo allo scolare. Deo gratias. Amen"

7. 59r „Qui si comincia lo capitolo delle proportione pertinente al contrapuncto
<P>roportioni in musica nelle quali consistono"

59v „. . . s'apartiene al capitolo delle proportioni"

[2] Published by J. Wolf in *Festschrift Kroyer*, 17-39.

THE TREATISE

The *Notitia del valore delle note* is a short elementary compilation of the principles of mensuralist notation, written in the Tuscan dialect. It is an *unicum*, copied in a manuscript (just described), which contains seven theoretical works, all written in the same tongue.

Date. The treatise was composed in the last years of the 14th or in the first years of the 15th century. The inclusion of hollow red notes, as well as the existence of the *modi maximarum*, taken into account for all the eight rhythmic modes defined in the work, leaves no doubt as to this date. Neither Marchettus nor Philippe de Vitry admits this large mensuration; indeed, the former very clearly denies it. Among the more important Italian writings, we find the mode mentioned for the first time in a work of Prosdocimus de Beldemandis, composed in the year 1412 [3]. The mode is also defined in French treatises probably compiled during the latter part of the 14th century. But inasmuch as the author of our compilation drew his material, as we shall see later, from the oral tradition of the Florentine school, and only secondarily from authoritative treatises, it would be imprudent to suppose that the teaching concerning the *modus maximarum* had become widespread in central Italy before the last quarter of the 14th century. Despite the reluctance of theorists to admit the existence of a new mode, the mensuration existed in fact in the works of Florentine musicians composed around the

[3] *Tractatus practice cantus mensurabilis ad modum Ytalicorum*, recently reedited by C. Sartori, *La Notazione italiana del trecento;* also in CS, 3, 228-248.

middle of the century. So we can safely declare that our author was referring to a practice that had already become "classic" at the moment these rules were formulated.

Hollow red notes, however, were quite unknown before the second half of the century. Those pieces of the Florentine school where they are to be found can in no case be dated earlier than 1375. Likewise, the theorists of the first part of the 14th century make no mention of them, and it is in such works as the *Tractatus de diversis figuris* of Filipotus de Caserta [4], composed towards the end of the century, that we find them explained for the first time.

The Tenors of two isorhythmic motets cited in the *Notitia* also confirm this date, for these compositions, *Sub Arturo* and *Ida Capillorum*, belong to the latter half of the 14th century.

Language. It is indeed most exceptional to find a mediaeval musical treatise written in the vulgate. Latin was then the traditional language for teaching, especially in the form of a written treatise, and even in the 16th century the number of works in other languages is not great. Therefore, if the Tuscan speech was used in this case for notational instruction, it was because the treatise — as in fact the entire manuscript from which it is taken — was compiled to answer the needs of a category of students who were not able to understand Latin. A brief inscription on the verso of the first fly-leaf of our codex offers a very probable explanation of why this volume contains writings in Italian only, and why the readers of these texts were not supposed to know Latin. The otherwise blank page in question bears the following *ex-libris* in an early 15th century hand, which is not, however, that of the

[4] CS, 3, 118-124.

scribe: "A uso di s̄r landomina" (or "laudomina", "laudonima", etc.: the letters between the *o* and *a* are formed by six disjoined vertical strokes, which can be read as *m*, *n*, *i*, *u*, in numerous combinations). So then, the manuscript belonged to a convent of nuns, one of the few literate classes whose education did not necessarily include the universal language of Christendom. As is well known, members of feminine religious orders were generally ignorant of the Church's official tongue, so much so that even in the 17th century special editions of liturgical books, particularly Breviaries, were printed for them, with all rubrics in the vulgate. Therefore, it is not surprising to find this codex entirely in Tuscan, and intended for the singers of some Florentine convent, who strove to embellish their ceremonies with counterpoint. It is also possible that the manuscript was used as a text-book for girls attending the convent to receive such education as was then given to the fair sex, and of which music was one of the usual subjects.

The style of the treatise attempts no show of elegance. The work is composed in colloquial Tuscan: grammatical incorrections abound and the syntax is so loose that in a few cases the exact meaning of the author is not altogether clear. The vocabulary and the spelling is the ordinary Tuscan usage of the late 14th- early 15th century. However, to the present writer's knowledge, many technical expressions contained in the work are not found elsewhere, and doubtless belong to the specifically Florentine musical terminology of the epoch. This unfamiliar mode of expression presents not a few original aspects of mensuralist problems, and is one of the chief interests of the treatise.

Frequent scribal errors both in text and musical examples (the latter transcribed?) warrant the hypothesis that the sole source of the treatise come down to us is not the archetype.

Our manuscript was evidently copied from a lost model by a scribe who, to judge from the mistakes, did not seem always to understand fully what he was reproducing (cf. the critical notes to the text). It is probable that the work was largely diffused in the early 15th century, inasmuch as it offered a rudimentary notational instruction to those who could not read Latin; above all, it must have been welcomed by many feminine religious institutions and by gentlewomen seeking an initiation in music. This circumstance further corroborates the date suggested above, because the somewhat corrupt state of our only extant copy is hardly due to the carelessness of one scribe, but is rather the result of numerous reproductions of the text.

THE THEORY

Plan of the work. As can easily be seen from the following schematic plan of the treatise, the author of the *Notitia* did not observe a very strict or logical order in presenting his material:

FIRST PART

A. **Figures of music**

- *1a* Le sei note
- *1b* Note perfecte et imperfecte
- *1c* Pose
- *1d* Legature

B. **The rhythmic modes**

1. *The 4 perfect modes*
   - *2* Modo perfecto suppremo
   - *3* Modo perfecto lato

4 Modo perfecto sublato
5 Modo perfecto stremo

2. *The 4 imperfect modes*
6 Modo imperfecto magiore
7 Modo imperfecto minore
8 Modo imperfecto stremo
8 Modo imperfecto substremo

C. **The prolations**
10 Prolatione perfecta
11 Prolatione imperfecta

SECOND PART

	Libellus cantus mensurabilis
12 Note perfecte et imperfecte	*1f*
13 Punti	*3*
14 Come le prolationi si dividono	
D. **Signs of measure**	
15 Segni di modo	*4*
16 Segni di prolatione	
E. **Various subjects**	
17 Sincopa	*7*
18 Pose	*8*
19 Diminutione	*9*
20 Segni di modo	*4a*
21 Colore o taglia	*10*

The incoherence of this order of presentation is the result of an attempt on the author's part to unite in his one short compilation the essentials of two other more important theories, of which the present work can be considered a summary. The material falls into two distinct groups, of which the second (*12-21*) is a fairly faithful reproduction of the plan of that widely known work the *Libellus cantus mensura-*

bilis, generally ascribed to Johannes de Muris, and whose concordances are given in the above plan. It is striking, however, that no chapter was devoted to Alteration (*LCM 2*), although it is frequently mentioned. Nos. 5 and 6 of the pseudo-Muris were omitted because their subjects — modes and ligatures — are discussed in the first part of the *Notitia;* likewise, Nos. *1a-1e* are covered in this same section. But the Tuscan theorist did not take the trouble to unite the two chapters on perfect and imperfect notes (*1b, 12*), rests (*1c. 18*) and modal mensuration signs (*15, 20*).

The first half of our treatise (*1-11*) is drawn from a source that the editor has not been able to identify. It is here that we find most of the peculiar features of this treatise, and it can safely be said that these chapters form the essential part of the work. The central subject of this section is the definition of the eight rhythmic modes. To be sure, these mensurations are in substance taught by all treatises that admit the *modi maximarum*, but their presentation here as well as their mensuration signs and names are quite new. Taking into consideration the bulk of treatises on notation of the late 14th and early 15th centuries, and the manner in which this modal theory is here expounded, one concludes that the real source of this part of our author's compilation was the oral tradition of Florentine pedagogy. The chief purpose of the present work would seem to be that of initiating the novice to the mensurations practised by musicians of the Florentine school where, as can be seen from the extant works of these men, the *modi maximarum* were frequently used [5]. This was a characteristic of the central Italian tradition. And the present

[5] Already in the works of the early Florentine composer, Gherardello, the *modus maior* is used in the majority of the compositions extant.

treatise is one of the earliest documents to base all modal mensuration on the *maxime*, for the *modi longarum* are simply not taken into account by our author.

Contents. The following is a synoptic analysis of the whole theory expounded by the *Notitia:*

Figures. Mensuralist notation takes into account 6 notes or figures: *max.*, *lo.*, *br.*, *sb.*, *min.*, and *semimin.* (*1a*, 1-7). There are two kinds of *semimin.*: 1. that worth one-half *min.* (*1a*, 8); 2. that worth one-third *min.*, that is, triplets (*1a*, 9).

Mensuration. All notes are subject to ternary and binary (perfect and imperfect) mensuration (*1b*, 1).

A perfect note contains three notes of the figure immediately following it, in the above-mentioned order (*1b*, 2-6; *13*, 6-7). *Max.* and *lo.* are always perfect in the perfect modes (*12*, 2, 7); *br.* and *sb.* are always perfect in perfect major prolation (*12*, 3); *br.* is always perfect in perfect minor prolation (*12*, 5) and *sb.* is always perfect in imperfect major prolation (*12*, 4).

Each and every note can be imperfected by any one of the notes of lesser value (*1b*, 9); by writing it hollow or in red, its value is diminished by one-third, if it be naturally perfect (*12*, 8). *Max.* and *lo.* are naturally imperfect in the imperfect modes; *br.* is naturally imperfect in imperfect major prolation (*13*, 8). But although this *br.* is imperfect because it contains but 2 *sb.*, inasmuch as it contains 6 *min.*, a perfect number being divisible by 3, it can be further imperfected by the subtraction of 1 or 2 *min.*; thus this *br.* is imperfect as regards its next lowest division (*sb.*), but perfect by reason of the number of *min.* it contains (*13*, 9-12). *Br.* and *sb.* are always imperfect in imperfect minor prolation (*12*, 6). *Min.*, imperfect by nature, can be perfected by a *pu. perf.* (*1b*, 6-7).

Semimin., the smallest division of rhythmic values, is worth one-half or one-third *min.*, depending upon its form (*1b*, 8).

Imperfect notes can be perfected by a dot, or by a mensuration sign (*12*, 9). According to Philippe de Vitry, when black notes are perfect, hollow or red notes are imperfect, and vice-versa (*12*, 10).

Rests. Each note has its corresponding rest of equal value (*1c*, 1). The number of spaces occupied by a rest indicates the number of *br.* it is worth (*1c*, 2-7). *Sb.*, *min.* and *semimin.* rests are formed similarly (*1c*, 8-10). Perfect rests replace perfect notes, and vice-versa (*1c*, 11). The rest cannot be perfected by a dot, as can the note; perfect and imperfect rests are indicated by their form (*1c*, 12). A *sb.* rest cannot figure in a syncopation of *min.* in the major prolation; a *br.* rest cannot be syncopated by a *sb.* in any prolation (*18*, 2).

Ligatures. Ligatures are composed of *max.*, *lo.*, *br.* and *sb.* (*1d*, 1-3). An ascending ligature without any stem is composed of *br.* only (*1d*, 4). An upward stem on the first element of a ligature makes *sb.* of the first 2 notes (*1d*, 5, 12). There can be no less and no more than 2 *sb.* in any ligature (*1d*, 6). A downward stem at the beginning of a ligature makes a *lo.* of the first note (*1d*, 7). If the first element of a descending ligature be square or oblique, and the last element square, these 2 notes are *lo.* (*1d*, 8). The *max.* can replace the *lo.* at these two points (*1d*, 9). If the last element be oblique, the note is *br.* (*1d*, 10). All intermediary elements are *br.* (*1d*, 11). A downward stem makes a *br.* of the first note (*1d*, 13).

Rhythmic modes (mensuration of *max.*, *lo.*, *br.* and *sb.*). Modes are perfect and imperfect (2, 1). There are 4 perfect modes (2, 2) and 4 imperfect modes (*6*). The perfect modes are called: 1. *suppremo*, 2. *lato*, 3. *sublato*, 4. *stremo* (2, 2). The imperfect modes are called: 1. *magiore*, 2. *minore*, 3. *stremo*, 4. *substremo* (*6-9*).

Modo perfecto suppremo. *Max.* = 3 *lo.*; *lo.* = 3 *br.*; *br.* = 3 *sb.*; *sb.* = 3 *min.* (2, 3-4). This is the largest possible mensuration (2, 5). *Max.* can be imperfected: = 2 *lo.* = 6 *br.* (2, 6-7). *Max.* can be further imperfected and contain only 5 *br.* (2, 8). If the *max.* however contain only 4 *br.*, it must be written hollow. The 2 remaining *br.* are placed immediately before or after this note (2, 9-10). If the *br.*, or their equivalents, which compensate the imperfection of the *max.*, are far removed from that note, it must then be written hollow in red (2, 11). Further imperfection of the *max.* is impossible (2, 12). The hollow black *max.* can also stand for 6 *br.*, if the 3 remaining *br.*, which compensate its imperfection, are far removed (2, 13).

Lo. can be imperfected by 1 *br.*; it then contains 2 *br.* = 6 *sb.* (2, 14-15). *Lo.* can contain only 5 *sb.* (2, 16). If the 6th *sb.* immediately precede or follow, the *lo.* is written in the usual way; if the *sb.* be far removed, then the *lo.* will be written hollow (2, 17-18). If the third *br.* of an imperfect *lo.* be far removed from it, then the *lo.* must be written hollow black, or full red (2, 19).

The *max.* can be imperfected by any note whatsoever, provided that the above-mentioned values are maintained, that is, provided the *max.* contain at least 4 *br.*, and that the imperfecting notes compensate at least 2 other *br.* (2, 20).

This mode is always in major prolation (*novenaria*) (2, 22). *Lo.*, *br.*, *sb.* and *min.* are subject to alteration (2, 23).

Modo perfecto lato. *Max.* = 3 *lo.*; *lo.* = 3 *br.*; *br.* =

2 *sb.*; *sb.* = 3 *min.* (*3*, 2). *Lo.*, *br.* and *min.* are subject to alteration (*3*, 3). The prolation is always major imperfect (*senaria imperfecta*), because the *br.* is binary (*3*, 4).

Modo perfecto sublato. *Max.* = 3 *lo.*; *lo.* = 3 *br.*; *br.* = 3 *sb.*; *sb.* = 2 *min.* (*4*, 2). *Lo.*, *br.* and *sb.* are subject to alteration (*4*, 3). Prolation is perfect minor (*senaria perfecta*), because the *br.* is ternary (*4*, 5).

Modo perfecto stremo. *Max.* = 3 *lo.*; *lo.* = 3 *br.*; *br.* = 2 *sb.*; *sb.* = 2 *min.* (*5*, 2). This is the shortest perfect mode in music (*5*, 3). *Lo.* and *br.* are subject to alteration (*5*, 4). Prolation is imperfect minor (*quaternaria*) because the *br.* is binary, composed of 4 *min.* (*5*, 5-7).

Modo imperfecto magiore. In this, and in all imperfect modes, *max.* = 2 *lo.*; *lo.* = 2 *br.* *Lo.* and *br.* are not subject to alteration (*6*, 2-4). In this first mode, *br.* = 3 *sb.*; *sb.* = 3 *min.* *Sb.* and *min.* are subject to alteration (*6*, 6-9).

Modo imperfecto minore. *Max.* = 2 *lo.*; *lo.* = 2 *br.*; *br.* = 2 *sb.*; *sb.* = 3 *min.* (*7*, 2, 4). Only the *min.* is subject to alteration (*7*, 3, 5).

Modo imperfecto stremo. *Max.* = 2 *lo.*; *lo.* = 2 *br.*; *br.* = 3 *sb.*; *sb.* = 2 *min.* (*8*, 2). Only the *sb.* is subject to alteration (*8*, 3). Only the *br.* can be imperfected (*8*, 6).

Modo imperfecto substremo. *Max.* = 2 *lo.*; *lo.* = 2 *br.*; *br.* = 2 *sb.*; *sb.* = 2 *min.* (*9*, 2).

Prolation (mensuration of *br.* and *sb.*). There are 4 prolations (*14*), of which two are perfect and 2 imperfect (*10*, 2): 1. *perfecto magiore*, 2. *perfecto minore*, 3. *imperfecto magiore*, 4. *imperfecto minore* (*10-11*, *14*).

Perfect major prolation. *Br.* = 3 *sb.*; *sb.* = 3 *min.* (*10*, 3-4); *14*, 2-3), called *nonario* by the Italians. Syncopation, diminution, hollow notes and dragma can be employed in this mensuration (*14*, 4).

Perfect minor prolation. *Br.* = 3 *sb.*; *sb.* = 2 *min.* (*10*, 5-6; *14*, 8-10), called *senaria perfecta* by the Italians. Syncopation, hollow and red notes can here be used (*14*, 11). The prolation is called „minor" because the *sb.* is imperfect, whereas this note is perfect in the major prolation (*10*, 8).

Imperfect major prolation. *Br.* = 2 *sb.*; *sb.* = 3 *min.* (*11*, 1-2; *14*, 5-6),called *senaria imperfecta* by the Italians. Syncopation, hollow notes and dragma can likewise here be used (*14*, 7).

Imperfect minor prolation. *Br.* = 2 *sb.*; *sb.* = 2 *min.* (*11*, 4; *14*, 12-14), called *quadernaria* by the Italians. Syncopation and the *pu. perf.* can here be used (*14*, 15). This is the smallest mensuration used in music (*11*, 5).

Duality of mensuralistic signs. In music, every sign, figure or mensuration is of two kinds (*13*, 1). There are two kinds of *max.*, *lo.*, *br.*, *sb.* and *min.*: perfect and imperfect (*13*, 2). There are two kinds of modes, equally perfect and imperfect (*13*, 3). There are two kinds of dots: *pu. div.*, and *pu. perf.* (*13*, 4).

Punctus perfectionis. This dot perfects the imperfect note after which it is placed (*13*, 5). According to French technique, any imperfect note may be perfected by such a dot (*14*, 16).

Punctus divisionis. This dot is placed between two notes, of which one is to be altered: 2 *lo.* between *max.*; 2 *br.* between *lo.*; 2 *sb.* between *br.*; 2 *min.* between *sb.* (*13*, 14-17: this theory is, as explained below, the exact reverse of the correct definition).

Syncopation. Syncopation interrupts the normal order of mensuralist calculation: an imperfect red or hollow note in perfect mensuration is to be set aside until the values which compensate its imperfection be found, generally at the end of a series of notes (*17*, 1-5).

Diminution. The diminished *max.* becomes a *lo.*, the *lo.* a *br.*, the *br.* a *sb.*, the *sb.* a *min.*, the *min.* a *semimin.* This applies to the corresponding rests (*19*, 1). In perfect mode and imperfect *tempus*, a diminished *lo.* will be worth 3 *sb.* (*19*, 2). In perfect mode and *tempus*, values are diminished by one-third (*19*, 3).

Color and talea. *Color* is a series of notes and rests whose rhythmic values are repeated one or more times in different melodies (*21*, 1). *Talea* is another term for *color*, applied to motet Tenors (*21*, 2). If the *talea* were repeated in the same melody, it would be equivalent to a refrain sung over and over again (*21*, 4).

Mensuration signs. As has been said, the central feature of the treatise is the modal theory, whose definition is accompanied by a set of mensuration signs which, so far, have not been encountered in any manuscript containing musical works. This is an eloquent indication of the fact that a large number of sources of 14th-century music has perished, for it would be difficult to believe that a treatise whose aim was to popularise the most elementary principles of notation would carry signs which were never used by composers. We may be sure that they were commonly employed in Florence during the 14th century. Some vestige of closely related, but not identical, semeiology can be found in two Florentine manuscripts, **P**

and **Pal** [6]. The following list reproduces in rational order all the mensuration signs cited in the present treatise, whether indicating the mode or the prolation [7].

Sign	Significance	Name in Notitia	Where cited
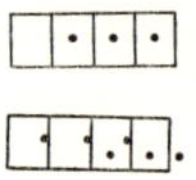	Modus maior perfectus, modus minor perfectus, tempus perfectum, prolatio maior	Modo perfecto suppremo	*2*, 21; *15*, 2. Ex. 22, 33 a-b, 40 a-b.
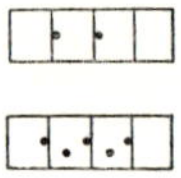	Modus maior perfectus, modus minor perfectus, tempus imperfectum, prolatio maior	Modo perfecto lato	*3*, 4; *15*, 3.
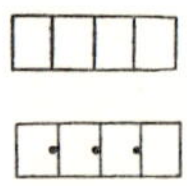	Modus maior perfectus, modus minor perfectus, tempus perfectum, prolatio minor	Modo perfecto sublato	*4*, 4; *15*, 4. Ex. 25.
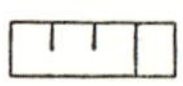	Modus maior perfectus, modus minor perfectus, tempus imperfectum, prolatio minor	Modo perfecto stremo	*5*, 5; *15*, 5. Ex. 26.
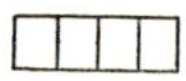	Modus minor perfectus	Modo perfecto (secundo Gian de Muris)	*20*, 4. Ex. 41a.
	Modus maior imperfectus, modus minor imperfectus, tempus perfectum, prolatio maior	Modo imperfecto magiore	*15*, 7. Ex. 27.
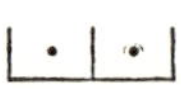	Modus maior imperfectus, modus minor imperfectus, tempus imperfectum, prolatio maior	Modo imperfecto minore	*15*, 8. Ex. 28.

[6] **P** 131v-132r (*Gloria* of Gherardello), 136v (*Sanctus* of Lorenzo); **Pal** 1v-2r (*Piu non mi curo* of Giovanni), 46v-47r (*Ita se n'era star* of Lorenzo), to mention but a few at random. The writer is not for the moment able to identify the basse dance treatise in which something similar occurs.

[7] These signs were published, but not without error, in *WCM*, 1, 99.

Sign	Significance	Name in Notitia	Where cited
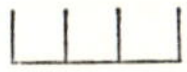	Modus maior imperfectus, modus minor imperfectus, tempus perfectum, prolatio minor	Modo imperfecto stremo	*15*, 9. Ex. 29, 32.
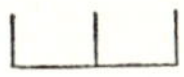	Modus maior imperfectus, modus minor imperfectus, tempus imperfectum, prolatio minor	Modo imperfecto sub-stremo	*15*, 10. Ex. 30.
	Modus minor imperfectus	Modo imperfecto (secundo Gian de Muris)	*20*, 5. Ex. 41b.
	Tempus perfectum, prolatio maior	Prolatione del perfecto magiore	*16*, 1. Ex. 35, 39a.
	Tempus perfectum, prolatio maior	Prolatione del perfecto magiore	*16*, 1. Ex. 22, 23, 33a, 40 b-c, 41b.
	Tempus perfectum, prolatio minor	Prolatione del perfecto minore	*16*, 7. Ex. 39c.
	Tempus perfectum, prolatio minor	Prolatione del perfecto minore	*16*, 8. Ex. 25, 29, 37, 39d.
	Tempus imperfectum, prolatio maior	Prolatione dello imperfecto magiore	*16*, 12. Ex. 39b.
	Tempus imperfectum, prolatio maior	Prolatione dello imperfecto magiore	*16*, 12. Ex. 28, 33b, 34c.
	Tempus perfectum, prolatio maior	Prolatione del perfecto minore (*sic*)	Ex. 39c.
	Tempus imperfectum, prolatio minor	Prolatione dello imperfecto minore	*16*, 13, 15. Ex. 39c, 41a.
	Tempus imperfectum prolatio minor	Prolatione dello imperfecto minore	*16*, 15. Ex. 26, 30, 39d.

Special vocabulary. While the greater part of the musical terminology used in the *Notitia* is a literal translation of the traditional Latin terms, a few words and expressions demand special notice, for they are here used in a peculiar sense, and some of them are, to the present author's knowledge, not to be encountered elsewhere in theoretical works.

Composita (*1*, 6) is employed in the sense of *ligatura cum opposita proprietate.*

Filo, used several times in the first part of the work (*1a*, 7; *1d*, 4, 5, 7, 12) always means *cauda*, that is, the stem of notes or ligatures.

Fusello (*14*, 7) designates the *dragma*, as used in Ex. 36, worth two *min.* This is manifestly an Italian translation of the French *fuisé* named in the Anon. III [8].

The most original terminology of the entire treatise is certainly that of the names given to the eight rhythmic modes, already cited in the preceding table: *lato, magiore, minore, stremo, sublato, substremo* and *suppremo.* The modes *maior* and *minor* are generally used by theorists, but not in the sense found in the present work. *Lato* is perhaps a translation of the Latin *largus*, while *stremo* probably renders *strictus.* It is more than probable that these terms are peculiar to the Florentine school.

Prolatione always means, in the *Notitia*, the mensuration of the *br.* and the *sb.*, and not simply of the *sb.* The designations *prolatione del perfecto magiore* or *minore*, and *prolatione dello imperfecto magiore* or *minore* are again special acceptations of terms in general use.

Separatione (*1c*, 1) or *spiratione* (*21*, 1) both mean

[8] In the Ms Paris, Bibl. nat., lat. 15128, fol. 128r, the correct reading is „fuisés" and not fuiscée as printed in *CS* 3, 373.

pausa. The first word is probably a scribal error for the second, because we find in the *LCM* (*8*, 1) the expression *aspiratio mensurata* [9].

Citations from other treatises. Only two authors are cited by the *Notitia*: Philippe de Vitry and the pseudo-Johannes de Muris. It is curious to note that both of these citations are of French origin, and that Marchettus and other Italian theorists are nowhere mentioned, nor is their special theory specifically referred to, save perhaps by the incidental use of one or two names of the Italian divisions of the *br.* (*nonario, senario imperfecto,* etc.).

Philippe de Vitry's authority is invoked concerning the relative significance of black and red notes (*12*, 10). The passage referred to is in the *Ars nova* [10].

The *LCM* is indirectly quoted twice, under the name of „Gian de Muris": 1. concerning the impossibility of syncopating the *sb.* rest in major prolation, and the *br.* rest in any prolation (*18*, 2)[11]; 2. the two mensuration signs for perfect and imperfect modes reproduced in *20*, 2-6 with somewhat unfavorable commentary, as variants of the mensuration signs peculiar to this treatise, are not quite identical with those given by the best manuscripts of the *LCM*, thus: 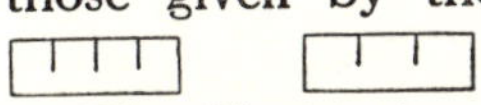 [12].

The *Notitia* is very decidedly partial to French notational theory. It entirely ignores the Italian theory of Marchettus and his followers; in the three cases where parallel nomen-

[9] *CS*, 3, 57.

[10] *CS*, 3, 21.

[11] *CS*, 3, 57.

[12] According to **Ashb B** 60v, Pi 25, **Mur Pal** 86v. **7369** fol. 5v gives still another variant, thus: 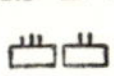 These are all different from signs reproduced in *CS*, 3, 54.

clature is referred to (*3*, 4; *4*, 5; *5*, 6), the *Tramontani* are mentioned in the first place. The *arte francesca* is specifically named a fourth time (*14*, 16), to say that this technique allows perfecting any imperfect note by means of a dot. But this French influence is in keeping with the Florentine school, whose notation was never that of Marchettus, but whose melodic inspiration was far more divergent from the French style thant that of the musicians who, like Bartolino, used the so-called Italian manner of mensuralistic art.

Erroneous theory. The elementary character of our treatise has caused its author to omit many important aspects of notational theory. The absence of any discussion of Alteration has been referred to above. In some cases the teaching of the Florentine theorist is confused and ambiguous, or even outright incorrect. Thus, the subjects of chapters *12* and *13* are very carelessly mixed, so that it would not be easy to rearrange them in a proper rational order. It is evident, however, that *13*, 8-13 belong to chapter *12*, despite the fact that this section was inspired by the preceding definition of the *pu. perf.* In the same chapter *13* we find only two *pu.* defined, instead of the usual four (*13*, 4). Perhaps here the author did not want to cite exception to his doctrine of the duality of all musical phenomena (*13*, *1*), which is itself a distinctly Italian and "modern" aspect of musical psychology. As is well known, the orthodox French theory, the very *autori musici passati* invoked in another part of the work (*2*, 1), always insisted upon the ternary nature of music and its notation. However, the theory of the *duplex punctus* already exists in the *LCM*, *3*, 1 [13].

The definition of the last element of the ascending ligature

[13] *CS*, 3, 53.

with an upward or downward stem (*1d*, 7 and Ex. 18, lig. 6) is not in accordance with the accepted interpretation of this figure. Further on it is declared (*13*, 16) that a *pu. div.* placed between two notes causes the alteration of the second, whereas in reality it prevents such an alteration.

Examples. It is in the musical examples that the most serious errors are found. In this detail, the *Notitia* is not unlike other treatises come down to us in corrupt sources. Probably, however, these mistakes are not due to the author of the work, but to careless copying by many scribes. Some of the examples show the reverse of what they propose to illustrate; others make little or no sense at all. In the present edition the editor has undertaken to correct those examples where the nature of scribal error could be reasonably surmised. In other cases the music in its distorted form has been left, as correction would have lead too far astray from the original.

Exs. 9, 12 and 13 are carelessly copied, and it is not always clear just how much the rests cover.

Ex. 18, first lig.: the downward stem on the last note does not appear in the manuscript, but the figure is in any event erroneous, as 2 *lo.* cannot follow in this way; second lig.: the first stem is at the left in the original; last lig.: here we have an oblique final, with an upward tail, designated as *lo.*

Ex. 20 contains a red hollow *max.* worth 6 *br.*, whereas is should stand for only 4.

Ex. 21 does not correspond to the text (*2*, 12-13), because both of the hollow *max.* are worth 4 *br.*, and not 6, as stated.

Ex. 22 carries a small *r* above the last hollow *lo.*, doubtless meaning "rosso" for the rubricist.

Ex. 23 does not include any case of an altered *lo.*

Exs. 27, 28 are incomplete, as the modal mensuration is not filled in.

Exs. 34 and 37 are quite incorrect, and do not appropriately illustrate the principle to which they supposedly refer. Nevertheless, the editor has not seen fit to correct these two lines, for reasons stated above.

Exs. 38 and 39d^2 do not complete the *tempus* mensuration.

Ex. 41a is the Tenor *Ante thronum trinitatis* of the motet *Ida Capillorum*, which will be discussed below.

Ex. 41b is incorrectly diminished, and certain notes have been omitted, but restored in the present edition.

The following list gives the object of each of the 43 examples cited in the treatise:

No.	OBJECT
1	Maxima
2	Longa
3	Brevis
4	Semibrevis
5	Ligatura cum opposita proprietate
6	Minima
7—8	Semiminima
9—10a	Pausae maximae
10bc	Pausae longae
11	Pausa brevis
12	Pausa semibrevis
13	Pausa minima
14	Pausa semiminima
15	Ligatura cum proprietate et sine perfectione
16	Ligatura cum opposita proprietate et cum perfectione
17	Ligatura sine proprietate et cum perfectione
18	Ligaturae variae
19	Imperfectio maximae ex parte propinqua
20	Imperfectio maximae (rubeae) ex parte remota
21	Imperfectio maximae vacuae ex partibus propinqua et remota
22	Imperfectio longae
23	Alteratio longae, brevis et semibrevis

24 Modus maior perfectus temporis imperfecti (*modo lato*)
25 Modus maior perfectus temporis perfecti (*modo sublato*)
26 Modus maior perfectus temporis imperfecti (*modo stremo*)
27 Modus maior imperfectus temporis perfecti prolationis maioris (*modo magiore*)
28 Modus maior imperfectus temporis imperfecti prolationis maioris (*modo minore*)
29 Modus maior imperfectus temporis perfecti prolationis minoris (*modo stremo*)
30 Modus maior imperfectus temporis imperfecti prolationis minoris (*modo substremo*)
31—32 Notae nigrae perfectae, vacuae et rubeae imperfectae, nigrae perfectae per signum
33 Punctus divisionis
34 Puncti divisionis et perfectionis in modo perfecto; in tempore perfecto maioris prolationis; in tempore imperfecto maioris prolationis
35 Tempus perfectum prolationis maioris (*prolatione perfecto magiore*)
36 Tempus imperfectum prolationis maioris (*prolatione imperfecto magiore*) cum notis vacuis et dragmis
37 Tempus perfectum prolationis minoris (*prolatione perfecto minore*) cum notis vacuis
38 Tempus imperfectum prolationis minoris (*prolatione imperfecto minore*)
39
a. tempus perfectum prolationis maioris (novenaria)
b. tempus imperfectum prolationis maioris (senaria imperfecta)
c. tempus perfectum prolationis minoris (*prolatione perfecta minore*)
d. tempus imperfectum prolationis minoris (*prolatione imperfecto minore*)

cum signis mensura
40 Sincopa maxima, longa, brevis (bis) et semibrevis vacuarum
41 Diminutio modorum perfecti et imperfecti 41a est prima talea tenoris *Ante thronum trinitatis*)
42—43 Talea tenorum de motetis: a. *Luce clarus;* b. *Sub Arturo;* c. *Omni habenti*

Tenors cited. Three isorhythmic motet Tenors have been named in the treatise, and the first *talea* of each reproduced as an example. A fourth Tenor is used but not named (Ex. 41a). Of these four works only two have come down to us: 1. the motet *Sub Arturo* — *Fons citharizantium* — T. *In omnem terram* of Alanus contained in **Ch** ff. 70v-71r and **BL** ff. 225v-226r and a fragment, No. 339; 2. the motet *Ida Capillorum* — *Porcio nature* — T. *Ante thronum trinitatis*, of Egidius Pusieux, contained in **Iv** ff. 6v-7r, **Ch** ff. 61v-62r, and the lost manuscript **Str** ff. 74v-75r (No. 122-123) and **Trém** ff. 2v-3r [14]. The two remaining works, *Luce clarus* and *Omni habenti* — probably the incipit of the *Tr* and not the title of the Tenor, to judge from the other citations — may, let us hope, some day be discovered in a manuscript yet to be brought to light.

[14] Ch. Van den Borren, *Le Manuscrit musical M. 222 C. 22 de la Bibliothèque de Strasbourg*, 129-134; H. Besseler in *AfM*, 8 (1926-1927), 236.

METHOD OF TRANSCRIPTION

The spelling of the unique source has been respected in all cases; however, the distinction between *u* and *v*, *i* and *j* has not been maintained. Punctuation and capital letters (only used for proper names and at the beginning of sentences) have been added. Diacritics have been employed only to distinguish between words of identical spelling: *e* and *é*, *anno* and *ánno*, etc. In these cases only the acute accent is used, to distinguish it from correct accentuation of modern Italian. A number in italics has been assigned to each chapter or division of text. Each sentence has likewise been numbered with small Arabic figures placed at the beginning. This numeration is begun anew in each chapter. Citations of the text are made by means of the chapter number, in italics, followed by the sentence numbers: e.g. *13*, 2, 6, refers to the second and sixth sentences of chapter 13. Besides the aforementioned number assigned to each chapter, subject words in the language of the treatise have also been added, printed for every chapter or division, in order to facilitate consultation of the text. These words are in italics, unless they are contained in the manuscript itself. Musical examples have been numbered in a continuous series and are referred to by their numbers.

All words added by the editor are in pointed brackets. One or more letters modified in a word are printed in italics; likewise, when omiting a letter, or letters, the letter preceding or following is printed in italics. Letters or words whose transcription is tentative, due to an unclear penstroke of the scribe, or to erasures or scribblings, are indicated by an asterisk placed near the lower part of the letter. A portion of the text considered as a scribal repetition or as an interpolation, and hence omitted in the transcription, is replaced by an asterisk printed near the upper part of the word preceding the omission. Similar asterisks also indicate two portions of text which have been rearranged in the transcription.

All modifications of the manuscript version are explained in the footnotes, which reproduce the rejected readings. Here Latin is used for uniformity with other works in the series. A second group of footnotes explains modifications made in the musical examples, but no typographical sign indicates these changes in the music itself. Red notes in the examples are within broken square brackets.

Citations from other treatises by the author are identified in the footnotes whenever possible.

Following the text of the treatise will be found a table of the chapters and an analytical index, composed by the editor in the language of the work itself. The titles given to the musical examples in the above table are in Latin, for the sake of general usage.

NOTITIA
DEL VALORE DELLE NOTE
DEL CANTO MISURATO

Re, fol. 13r

PER AVERE ALCUNA NOTITIA DEL VALORE DELLE NOTE DEL CANTO MISURATO ET DI LORO DIVISIONE

Ia
Figure del canto

1 Per che dico essere note del canto misurato sei, cioe maxima, longa, breve, semibreve, minima et semiminima.

2 La maxima puo essere formata absolutamente d'un corpo bilongo piu che largo. Exemplo:

Maxima

Ex. 1 

3 La longa che puo essere formata absolutamente in corpo quadro colla coda, come é qui per exemplo:

Longa

Ex. 2 

4 Breve absolutamente é un quadro, col filo o sença filo, come é qui per exemplo:

Brieve

Ex. 3 

5 Semibrieve é formata l'absoluta:

Semibrieve

Ex. 4

6 La composita é formata come nello exemplo si dimostra; et quando sono cosi composite o insieme legate, non possono essere meno di due ne piu. Exemplo:

Semibrieve composita

Ex. 5 

7 Minima é formata cosi col filo in su:

Minima

Ex. 6 

(13v) [8] Semiminima sono di due specie: la prima, che le due vagliono una minima. Exemplo:

Ex. 7 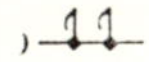 Semiminima

[9] L'altra, che tre vagliono .ii. minime. Exemplo:

Ex. 8  Semiminima

[10] Le due per una si chiama proportio duppla. [11] L'altre tre per due si dicono proportio sesquialtera.

1b *Quando sono le note perfecte et imperfecte*

[1] Hora le dicte note possono essere perfecte et imperfecte. [2] Et pero sara perfecta la maxima quando fia composta di tre longhe in un corpo, perfecte o imperfecte; la quale longha é sua proxima divisione. [3] Sara imperfecta quando fia composta di due longhe, perfecte o imperfecte. [4] Sara perfecta la longha quando di tre brevi perfecte o imperfecte in uno corpo sara composta; la quale breve é sua proxima divisione. [5] Sara perfecta la breve quando sara composta di tre semibrev*i* perfecte o imperfecte; la quale semibreve é sua proxima divisione. [6] Sara perfecta la semibreve quando sera in un corpo composta di tre minime; le quali minime naturalmente non possono essere altro che imperfecte. [7] Ma per força di punto dal lato dextro, saranno perfecte per tre semiminime, che per lo punto vagliono; si che seguita la minima essere proxima divisione della semibreve. [8] E della minima fia sua proxima divisione la semiminima, quando fia semiminima di tre per due, et quando fa semiminima di 2 per una. [9] Non é che ogni nota non possa essere divisione della maxima; et cosi della longa, ogni sua minore; et cosi della semibreve, la minima; et cosi della minima, la semiminima, **(14r)** come é detto.

1b: 5 semibrevi *ego*: -ve *cod.*

1c
Pose

[1] Anno ancora le supradette note el medesimo valore nelle pose o seperationi, le quali pose vogliono essere di tempo tanto, quanto sella nota si pronuntiasse. [2] Et per tanto la posa della maxima perfecta nel modo perfecto occupera tanti spatii, quanti tempi — cioe brievi — essa maxima varra. [3] Se sara d*i* no*ve* temp*i*, vuole la sua posa essere come é qui posto per exemplo qui di sotto:

Ex. 9a

[4] Se vara .vi., cosi:
Ex. 9b

o cosi:
Ex. 9c

[5] Se sara di quatro tempi, sara di .iiii. spatii, cosi:
Ex. 10a

[6] Se sara di tre, cosi:
Ex. 10b

[7] Se sara di dua, cosi:
Ex. 10c

[8] Se sara d'una, cosi:
Ex. 11

breve. [9] Della semibreve:
Ex. 12
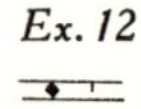
[10] Della minima:
Ex. 13
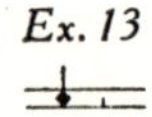

[11] Della semiminima:
Ex. 14
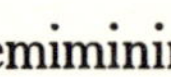

[12] Et nota che sella nota per cui tu farai la posa sara perfecta, la posa ancora sara cosi, et sella nota sara imperfecta, cosi sara la posa. [13] Ora per che ogni imperfecta puo essere perfecta per puncto dal lato dextro, non pero per punto puo la posa essere perfecta, ma perfecta et imperfecta puo essere secundo la perfectione o imperfectione della nota per cui é posta. [14] Et delle pose basti.

1d
Legature

[1] Avendo delle note absollute, et di loro forma et pose, bisogna vedere el loro valore et nome quando sono legate et

1c: 3 di nove *ego*: don *cod.* 4 *posita sub exemplo cod.* — .vi. *ego*: vi *cod.* 5 .iiii. *ego*: iiii *cod.* 6-7 *posite sub exemplo cod.*

Exempla: 9 *tres partes super una scala continua cod.* 10 *tres partes super una scala continua cod.* 12 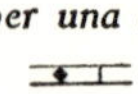 *cod.* 13 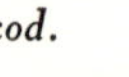 *cod.*

copulate insieme. 2 Et pero notisi che delle sei note di misura sopradette, le quatro prime si possono congiongere insieme et legare. 3 Et in quelle legature possonsi legare maxima con longha, longha con brieve, brieve con semibreve, et cosi per lo contrario, come di sotto per li exempli si vedra.

4 Adunqua ogni legatura asscendente mancan-**(14v)**-do d'ogni filo, tutte seranno brievi, come l'exemplo é qui:

Ex. 15  brevi

5 Ma sella prima avesse filo in su, sarebbe semibreve. 6 Et nota tale semibreve non puo essere sola, ne insieme piu che due. 7 Et se l'ultima avesse filo in su o in giu, sarebbe longa. Exemplo:

Ex. 16 

8 Item, ogni legatura descendente comminciando in corpo quadro o in corpo obliquo, sempre la prima et l'ultima rimanendo in corpo quadro, sara longha. 9 Et se sara in corpo bilongho, sara maxima. 10 Ma se l'ultima rimane in corpo obliquo, sara brieve. Exemplo:

Ex. 17 

11 Ma nota, cio che sara in meço tra l'ultima ella prima sara brieve. 12 Ma sella prima ara filo in su, saranno le prime due semibrievi. 13 Et se ara filo in giuso, sara brieve.

14 Seguita l'exemplo di legature insieme congiunte, asscendenti et discendenti miste con nota o copulate, facendo a ogni nota che debba essere longha uno .l., per piu agevolmente cognoscerla. Exemplo del detto:

Ex. 18 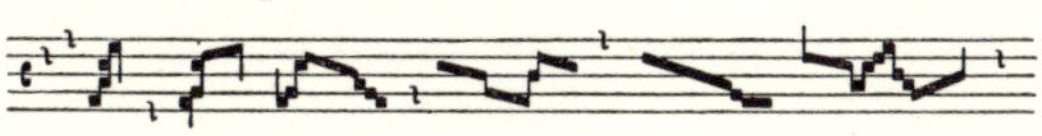

Id: 2 note *ego*: -ti *cod.* 11 *in marg. cod.*

Exemplum 18 *om. cod. cauda primae lig.*; *cauda secundae lig. a sinistra.*

QUANTI SONO *I* MODI

2
4 Modi perfecti [1] Veduto el valore delle note nelle legature semplicemente, é da vedere come s'adoperano secundo due modi veduti et trovati per li nostri autori musici passati. [2] Et per tanto notisi essere quatro modi da comporre note: el primo si dice modo perfecto suppremo; el secundo si dice modo perfecto lato; el terço modo si dice modo perfecto sublato; el quarto modo si dice modo perfecto stremo.

Modo perfecto suppremo [3] Ora modo suppremo si vu*o*le intendere quando il componitore **(15r)** d'un canto vuole che sia sua natura la maxima vaglia tre longhe, che la longha vaglia tre briev*i*, dove tre brievi faranno una perfectione et numerasi a tre brievi per volta. [4] Et allora tal canto sara di modo perfecto suppremo, et allora la maxima varra tre perfectioni, che verra a valere nove briev*i* che varranno tre longhe, et la brieve tre semibrievi, et la semibrieve tre minime. [5] Et non puo essere magior modo.

[6] Ora la maxima, che *é* perfecta in si facto modo puo essere imperfecta, cioe trarne la terça parte, che viene a valere due perfectioni, le quali sono sei brievi, il qual numero é perfecto, del quale si potrebbe ancora di quella perfectione trarne il terço. [7] Ma per che vi sia dentro il numero perfecto, non é pero la maxima perfecta, in quanto non é se non due di quelle che son sua proxima divisione. [8] Ma per che v'é dentro il sei, che é numero perfecto, se ne puo ancora trarre una brieve et rimanere la maxima nel suo corpo bilongho et naturale. [9] Ma se si volesse trarne il terço di quegli sei, puossi, faciendo la maxima vota (come ti mostro per exemplo sequente), et sussequentemente dinançi o dirieto porre el resto della sua

Titulus i *ego*: e *cod.* 3 vuole *ego*: vule *cod.* brievi *ego*: -ve *cod.* 4 brievi *ego*: -ve *cod.* 6 che é *ego*: che de *cod.*

perfectione. [10] Et intendesi essere imperfecta in tutto da parte propinqua:

Ex. 19 

[11] Ma sella maxima, imperfecta in tutto, avesse le sue compagne — che ánno a compiere la sua perfectione — di lungi, allora vuole essere rossa vuoita, come per exemplo si dimostra:

Ex. 20 

(15v) [12] E piu se volesse imperficere non si puo, volendo che rimanesse in corpo di maxima. [13] Ancora la maxima nera vuoita che vale iiii° per la imperfectione, che l'á propinqua, puo valere sei* ella avere remota cioe di longi. Exemplo:

Ex. 21 

[14] Come é dicto della maxima, cosi aviene della longha, quando é perfecta di tre brievi perfecte; la quale longha si puo imperficere, traendone la terça parte. [15] Et allora rimane la longha valente due brevi, che vagliono sei semibrievi, el quale numero é perfecto, donde che per sei si puo tripartire. [16] Che ancora la supradicta longha si puo piu inperficere, et vale cinque semibrievi. [17] Et s'ell'á appresso le parti dinançi o dirieto, puo starsi nel suo corpo di longha naturale. [18] Ma se á le sue parti che abbino a compiere la sua perfectione, bisogna essere nera voita, se sono rimote. [19] Ancora avendola imperfecta il terço* et avendo le compagne rimote, si fa nera voita, o rossa o piena. Exemplo:

Ex. 22 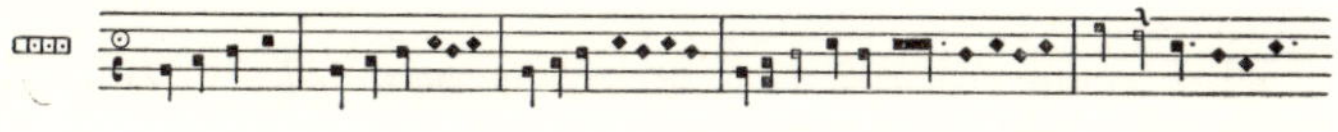

13 per . . . sei *bis scripta cod.* 15 semibrievi *ego*: -ve *cod.* 19 terço: *forte* terso *cod.*

[20] Ma per che é *si* detto et nominato di che note la maxima puo essere imperfecta, non si guardi pure a quelle, pero che puo essere imperfecta da ogni nota, pure che sieno tante che abbino el valore di quelle di che s'é dicto. [21] *E'* segno di questo modo suppremo un quadro con tre verg*o*le dentro, in questo modo: 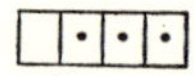 o cosi: 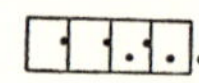. a significare che la bre-**(16r)**-ve vale tre semibrievi. [22] Et notisi questo modo non poter essere in altra prolatione che nel perfecto maggiore, cioe nel nonario. [23] Nel detto modo alterano le longhe, le brevi, le semibrevi et le minime. Exemplo:

Ex. 23

[24] E' da notare che per volere retrovare una perfectione di maxima, si vuole dividere ogni modo perfecto tre longhe per perfectione et tre brievi per longha. [25] Et allora sara trovata della maxima la sua perfectione. [26] Et cosi della longha, si che dunche si parte la maxima per longhe, et la longha per brievi o per loro valore, come di sopra si puo vedere.

DEL SECUNDO MODO

3 Modo perfecto lato [1] L'altro modo, cioe el secundo, si dice modo perfecto lato. [2] Et questo tale modo sara quando la maxima varra tre longhe, che la longha vaglia tre brievi, che la brieve vaglia due semibrievi, che la semibrieve vaglia tre minime. [3] Altera-no in questo modo le longhe, le brievi et le minim*e*. [4] El segno suo é un quadro con tre vergole o vero semibrievi, chelle

20 si *ego*: se *cod.* non si ... perfecta *in marg. cod.* 21 é *ego*: et *cod.* vergole *ego*: -gale *cod.* semibrievi *ego*: -ve *cod.*
3: 3 minime *ego*: -mi *cod.* 4 semibrievi *ego*: -ve *cod.*

Exemplum 23: 5[11] *max. cod.*

due sianno pontate in questo modo: 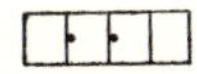 o in questo modo: 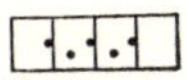 a significare chella brieve, cioe el ponto, vale due semibrievi perfecte, si che el quadrangulo cosi fatto significa il modo, et due virgole pontate significano la prolatione; [5] la quale prolatione secundo gli tramontani si dice imperfecto magiore, et secundo i taliani si dicie senario imperfecto — inperfecto in quanto si divide el tempo in due parti: tre et tre, sei. Exemplo: **(16v)**

Ex. 24 

DEL TERÇO MODO

[1] Vuolsi seguire el terço modo. [2] Et pero terço modo perfecto fia quando la maxima varra tre longhe, che la longha vaglia tre brievi, che la brieve vaglia tre semibrievi, che la semibrieve vaglia due minime. [3] Alterano in questo modo le longhe, le brievi, le semibrievi. [4] Dicesi questo modo: modo sublato perfecto, et il segno suo é uno quadro con tre vergole sança ponti, o tre semibrievi sança punto, in questo modo: 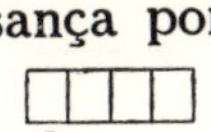 o cosi: 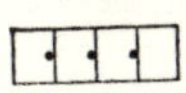 a significare el modo. [5] E le vergole, o tre semibrevi, significano la prolatione; la quale prolatione secundo i tramontani si dice perfecto minore, et secundo i taliani si dice senario perfecto, in quanto si divide el tempo in tre parti, dicendo: due et due, quatro, et due fa sei. Exemplo del dicto:

4 Modo perfecto sublato

Ex. 25 

DEL QUARTO MODO

[1] Seguita el quarto modo perfecto. [2] Et pero quarto modo perfecto fia quando la maxima varra tre longhe, chella longha vaglia tre brievi, che la brieve vaglia due semibrevi, et chella

5 Modo perfecto stremo

semibrieve vaglia due minime. [3] Dicesi questo modo: modo perfecto stremo, in quanto non sia formata nella *musica* pratica minor modo. [4] Alterano in questo modo stremo le lunghe et le brevi. [5] Et il segno suo é uno quadrangulo con tre vergole: [׀ ׀] **(17r)** non compiute <due del> le quali tre vergole. [6] Le due non compiute* significano la prolatione; la quale prolatione secundo gli tramontani si dice imperfecto minore, et secundo i taliani si dice quadernario, in quanto quatro minime vanno per un tempo, cioe per breve. [7] Dividesi el tempo in due parti, dicendo: .ii. et .ii., 4. Exemplo:

Ex. 26 

DE' QUATRO MODI IMPERFECTI ET DEL PRIMO

6 *4 Modi imperfecti* — [1] Veduto sub brevita di quatro modi perfecti, é da dire alcuna cosa de' modi imperfecti. [2] Et pero notisi, modo imperfecto sara quello che la maxima si dividera in due longhe imperfecte. [3] Et in tali modi non alterano né longhe né brievi. [4] Et la longha si dividera in due brievi. [5] L'altre note minori si dividino et alterano secundo in quale prolatione el canto é formato.

Modo imperfecto magiore — [6] Se é formato di perfecto magiore, alterano le semibrevi et le minime. [7] Sara el segno uno quadrangulo imperfecto, che significa el modo essere imperfecto, con due vergole fatto; e nel quadrangulo tre spatii puntati, che significano tre semibrevi perfecte, et tre spatii significano la prolatione. [8] Dividesi il tempo in tre semibrevi perfecte. [9] Dicesi questo modo: modo imperfecto magiore. Exemplo:

Ex. 27 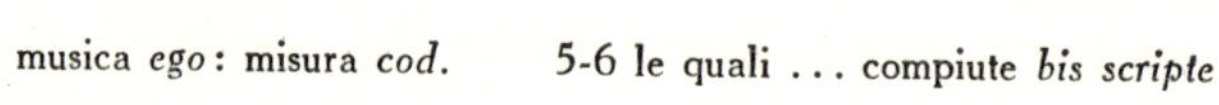

5: 3 musica *ego*: misura *cod.*   5-6 le quali . . . compiute *bis scripte in cod.*

DEL SECUNDO MODO IMPERFECTO

[1] Secundo modo imperfecto si dira modo imperfecto minore. [2] Varra la maxima due longhe, la longha due brevi, la **(17v)** brieve due semibrievi, la semibrieve tre minime. [3] Non alterano né longhe, né brevi, né semibrevi. [4] La longha si divide in due brevi, la breve in due semibrevi, la semibreve in tre minime. [5] Alterano in tal modo solamente le minime. [6] Sara il segno suo un quadrangulo imperfecto cum una vergola nel meço et in ogni spatio un punto. [7] El quadrangulo significa il modo imperfecto, due spatii significano dividersi el tempo in due semibrevi perfecte. *Exemplo: 7 *Modo imperfecto minore*

Ex. 28 

DEL TERÇO MODO IMPERFECTO

[1] El terço modo imperfecto si dira modo imperfecto stremo. [2] Varra la maxima due longhe et la longha due brievi, la brieve tre semibrevi, la semibreve due minime. [3] Altera in questo modo solamente la semibreve. [4] Dirassi questo modo: modo imperfecto stremo. [5] Sara il segno suo uno quadrangulo imperfecto no*n* intero cum due vergole, perche é ve dentro tre spatii sança punto, che significano quegli tre spacii dividersi il tempo in tre semibrevi imperfecte. [6] Et notisi in questo modo non potere imperficere altro che le brevi, pero che *é* perfecta di tre semibrevi. Exemplo: 8 *Modo imperfecto stremo*

Ex. 29 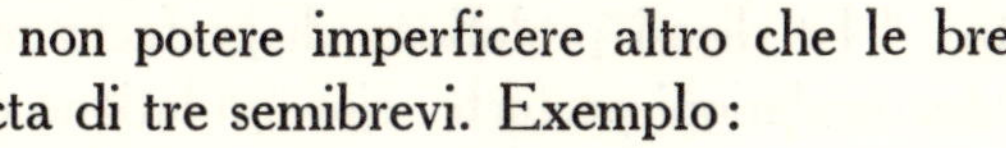

8: 5 non *ego*: no *cod.* 6 é *ego*: de *cod.* exemplo *ante* et notisi *cod.*

DEL QUARTO MODO

9 *Modo imperfecto substremo* [1] El quarto modo imperfecto si dera modo imperfecto substremo. [2] Varra la maxima due longhe, la longha due brevi, la breve due semibrevi, la semibreve due minime, si che in questo modo naturalmente tutte le note vi sono imperfecte. [3] Sara **(18r)** il segno del dicto modo uno quadrangulo imperfecto cum una vergola in meço, sança alcuno punto nelli spatii, a significare quegli due spatii dividersi el tempo in due semibrevi imperfecte. Exemplo:

Ex. 30 

[4] E questo basti per dimostratione de' modi imperfecti et de' loro segni.

QUANTE SIENO LE PROLATIONI

10 *Prolatione perfecta* [1] Hora quante sono le prolationi é da dirne. [2] Et pero notisi le prolationi essere due, cioe perfecta et imperfecta. [3] La prolatione perfecta sara quando d'un canto la breve si pronuntia di note perfecte, cioe di semibrevi perfecte, si come si pronuntia el nonario. [4] Et dirassi prolatione di perfecto magiore. [5] Sara ancora un' altra prolatione perfecta in quanto la breve vale tre semibrevi; ma sono tali semibrevi imperfecte, cioe di due minime l'una, si come si pronuntia el senario perfecto. [6] Et dicesi prolatione di perfecto minore; si che abiamo due prolationi perfecte, cioe prolatione di perfecto magiore et prolatione di perfecto minore. [7] Ciascuna é prolatione perfecta in quanto el tempo si parte et pronuntia

9: 2 semibrevi *ego*: -ve *cod.*
10: 6 prolationi *ego*: -ne *cod.*

per tre semibrevi. [8] Ma é detta la prima: prolatione perfecto magiore, per che le semibrevi sono perfecte; l'altra é ditta minore, per che le semibrevi sono imperfecte.

DELLA PROLATIONE IMPERFECTA

[1] La prolatione imperfecta sara quella quando la breve si pronuntia di due note perfecte, cioe di semibrevi, si come si pronuntia el senario imperfecto. [2] Et allora si dira prolatione d'imperfecto magiore. [3] Et abiamo la prolatione perfecta et et imperfecta magiore. [4] La prolatione imperfecta minore **(18v)** sara quando il tempo, cioe le brev*i*, si pronuntiano di note imperfecte, cioe di semibrevi imperfecte, si come si pronuntia il quadernario. [5] Dicesi prolatione d'imperfecto minore per che non c'é minor tempo di prolatione che il quadernario, el qual tempo é formato di due semibrevi imperfecte. *11 Prolatione imperfecta*

[6] Et delle prolationi basta.

QUALI SIANO LE NOTE PERFECTE O IMPERFECTE DI LOR NATURA

[1] Avengha che ne' supradicti iiii° modi sia dicto come la nota perfecta possa imperficere, pure bisogna dichiarare quali siano perfecte o imperfecte per lor natura. [2] Et pero nasce che ne' modi perfecti sempre é la maxima perfecta, et cosi la longha. [3] Nasce la breve et la semibreve nella prolatione del perfecto magiore sempre perfecta. [4] Nasce la semibreve nella prolatione dello imperfecto magiore sempre perfecta. [5] Nasce la breve nella prolatione del perfecto minore sempre perfecta. [6] Nasce nella prolatione dello imperfecto minore ogni sua nota imperfecta. [7] Ma di modo perfecto, la maxima et la longha nascono perfecte come di supra é dicto. *12 Note perfecte et imperfecte*

11: 4 brevi *ego*: -ve *cod.*

[8] Et é da notare, ogni nota perfecta si puo imperficere per vacuita o rosseça, o per trarne note o valore che sia il terço di quella che si vuole imperficere, come gia di sopra ne' modi perfecti s'é bona parte dicto. [9] Cosi ancora la nota che nasce imperfecta puo perficere per punto o per cifra. [10] Et Filippo de Vitriaco dice cosi, che quando le note nere sono perfecte, le voite o le rosse sianno imperfecte, et cosi per lo contrario; et per cotal modo le perfecte vengono imperfecte et le imperfecte vengono perfecte [a]. Exemplo:

Ex. 31

(19r) [11] Cosi ancora ne' tenori de' mottetti, quando le note ne' modi perfecti fossono nere perfecte*, le rosse sarebbono de' modi imperfecti, o veramente le voite, o veramente pur nere col segno del modo imperfecto. *Exemplo:

Ex. 32

DE' PUNTI ET QUANTI SIANO

13 Punti [1] Ancora é da vedere e da notare come questa musica pratica si parte ogni suo membro in due in questo modo: [2] la maxima é di due spetie, cioe perfecta et imperfecta; cosi due longhe, cosi due brevi, cosi due semibrevi, et cosi due minime. [3] Subsequentemente abbiamo due modi: modo perfecto et modo imperfecto.

[4] Seguendo cosi abiamo due punti: <punto> di divisione et punto di perfectione. [5] Punto di perfectione sara quando una nota di sua natura imperfecta, cioe quando varra due delle sue minori proxime, et allora ponendoli un punto dal

[a] *AN*, 12-13; publ. *CS*, 3, 21.

12: 11 perfecte *bis cripta cod.* exemplo *post* voite *in cod.*

lato dextro diventa perfecta. [6] Et ogni nota che é perfecta sempre vale tre della sua proxima divisione in questo modo: [7] la maxima á per sua proxima divisione la longha, la longha la brieve, la brieve la semibreve, la semibreve la minima, la minima la semiminima. [8] Sono imperfecte naturali ne' modi imperfecti la maxima et la longha; sono imperfecte naturali le brevi nello imperfecto magiore. [9] Et é imperfecta questa breve secundo la sua divisione, in quanto si divida in due semibrevi. [10] Ora, questa breve, quantunche sia imperfecta per la sua divisione, ancora puo piu imperficere in questo modo: [11] ella vale sei minime; sei é numero chi si puo tripartire equalmente, et ogni numero tripartitio equali si dice perfecto, si che secundo tale divisione si puo **(19v)** dire perfecta in secundo grado. [12] Et allora é conceduto per gli autori potersi imperficere per una o due minime; et a questo modo tale breve é imperfecta secundo la proxima divisione, et é perfecta secundo il numero delle minime che ella vale. [13] Delle perfecte et imperfecte sia ditto abastança, conchiudendo chelle perfecte sono come di sopra ne' modi s'é dicto; et cosi delle imperfecte et del punto che genera perfectione sia detto.

[14] Ora del punto di divisione segue. [15] Et pero é da notare che il punto di divisione si cognosce per due modi: [16] et prima, quando di due note ne dovesse alterare l'una et uno punto sia posto infra quelle due, é punto di divisione. [17] Et cosi si vuole intendere delle longhe tra le maxime, come delle brevi tralle longhe, o chome delle semibrevi tralle brevi, et cosi delle minime tralle semibrevi. Exemplo:

Ex. 33

13: 6 é *ego*: de *cod*. 12 et é *ego*: et de *cod*.

[18] Seguita alcuno exemplo di divisione; et dove é il punto, puo perficere o dividere si nel modo et nelle prolationi. [19] Et primo di modo perfecto nella magior prolatione perfecta. Exemplo: **(20r)**

Ex. 34

Exemplo del modo

Exemplo della prolatione magiore perfecta

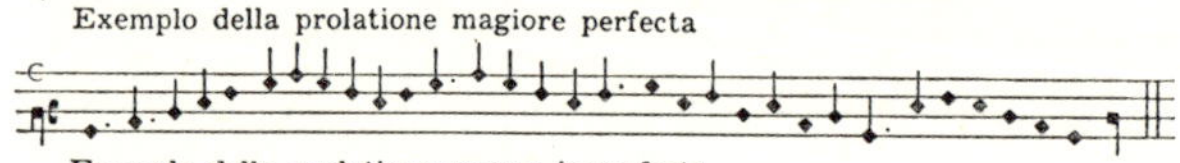

Exemplo della prolatione magna imperfecta

14
Come le prolationi si dividono

[1] Veduto le parti delle prolation*i* et la forma delle note et le legature et modi et loro valore di perfectione et imperfectione, etiamdio veduto de' punti, avengha che succintamente é da vedere come le prolationi nella divisione si conduchino, cioe come si dividono; le quali sono iiii°. [2] Et pero la prolatione del perfecto magiore fia per tempo tre semibrevi de tre minime l'una, si che verra a valere el tempo (cioe la breve) nove minime. [3] Dividesi il tempo in tre parti, dicendo: tre et tre, sei, et tre, nove, a semibrevi o val*o*re di semibrevi. [4] Poss*o*n essere nella conpositione del canto sincope et punti, riductioni di note, come nello exemplo bona parte se ne vede, come si pronuntia et sogle il maestro:

Ex. 35

14: 1 prolationi *ego*: -ni *cod.* 3 valore *ego*: -ere *cod.* 4 posson *ego*: -sun *cod.*

Exemplum 34a *pu. post 13 def. cod.* 34b *pu. post 21 def. cod.* 34c *18 min. cod.; pu. post 25 def. cod.*

[5] La prolatione dello imperfecto magiore sara per tempo (cioe per breve) due semibrevi di tre minime l'una, si che verra a valere il tempo (cioe la breve) sei minime l'una. [6] Dividesi il tempo in due parti, dicendo: tre et tre, sei, a semibrevi o valore di semibrevi. [7] Puovisi sincopare con punti et sança, et per vacuita et per fusello, e cosi nella prima prolatione, posto che non vi si dicesse. Exemplo:

Ex. 36

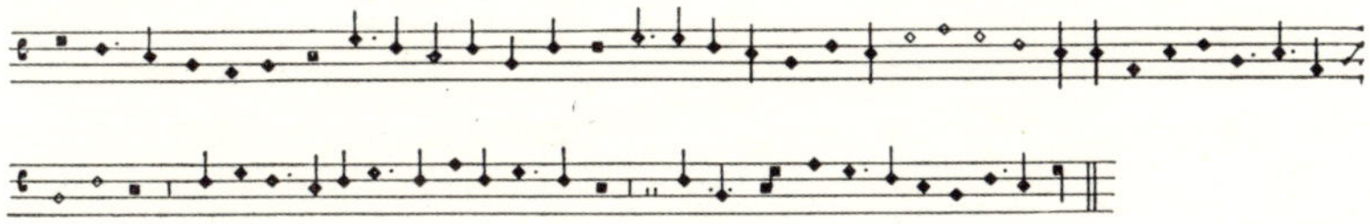

[8] La terça prolaione si dice perfecto minore. [9] Sara per tempo (cioe per breve) tre semibrevi imperfecte o loro valore, si che verra a valere el tempo sei minime. [10] Dividesi il tempo in tre parti, dicendo: due et due, quatro, et due, sei: minime s'intende o valore. [11] Puossi sincopare questa prolatione per punti, per vacuita et per rosseça, come l'exemplo ne fa parte de dimostratione: **(21r)**

Ex. 37

[12] La quarta prolatione si dice imperfecto minore. [13] Per tempo sara due semibrevi imperfecte o loro valore, si che varra il tempo iiii° minime o loro valore. [14] Dividesi el tempo

14: 5 semibrevi *ego*: -ve *cod.* 9 semibrevi *ego*: -ve *cod.*

Exemplum 37 *pu. def. post 10 cod.*

in due parti, dicendo: due et due, quatro minime o loro valore. 15 Puossi sincopare questa prolatione per punti, perficiendo le note, come in buona parte l'exemplo dimostra, et ancora sança punti:

Ex. 38

16 E' da notare che ogni nota imperfecta, o sua natura o per accidente, per punto puo perficere secundo l'arte francesca.

DE' SEGNI COME SI COGNOSCONO NEL MODO O LA PROLATIONE SANÇA DIVIDERE

15
Segni di modo

1 *I* canti sono formati d'alcuno modo perfecto de' dicti di sopra o d'alcuna delle supradicte prolationi. 2 Et pero, come **(21v)** é ditto, el segno del modo suppremo (che *é* il magiore) é formato cosi: 3 El segno del modo lato é formato cosi: 4 El segno del modo sublato é formato cosi: 5 El segno del modo perfecto stremo é formato cosi: 6 Cosi ancora, come sono iiii° modi imperfecti, si faranno illor segni. 7 Et per il primo modo imperfecto á el suo segno cosi: 8 El segno del secundo modo imperfecto é cosi: 9 El segno del terço modo cosi: 10 El segno del quarto modo cosi: 11 *I* nomi de' modi dinançi s'é dicto, per che seguita delle prolationi el cognoscerle mediante *i* segni dati da' nostri auctori antichi.

15: 1 i *ego*: e *cod.* 2 che é *ego*: che de *cod.* 6 come *ego*: -mo *cod.* 11 i *ego*: e *cod.* i segni *ego*: e se- *cod.*

COME SI COGNOSC*ONO* LE PROLATION*I* MEDIANTE ILLOR SEGNI

[1] E per tanto la prolatione del perfecto magiore á per suo segno un cerchio con tre punti dentro, o cum uno punto, in questo modo: ⊙ ⊙ [2] El cerchio significa prolatione et tre punti significan la divisione che il tempo si divide in* tre semibrevi perfecte. [3] El cerchio cum uno punto é posto a differentia d'uno cerchio che si fa perfecto minore, come si dira. [4] Et pero, quando si vuole seguire la prolatione del magior perfecto, si fa l'una de' supradicti segni. *16 Segni di prolatione*

[5] La prolatione del perfecto minore á per suo segno un cerchio con due punti. [6] Due punti significano che il tempo si divide per semibrevi imperfecte. [7] El cerchio intero significa el perfecto, a questo modo: ⊙ [8] A ancora per segno el cerchio solamente et sança punto, a differença del cerchio del magiore perfecto, che á un punto. L'exemplo del dicto: ○

[9] La prolatione dello imperfecto magiore á per suo segno uno meço cerchio con due punti che abia le corna a mano dextra. [10] Due punti significano **(22r)** il tempo dividersi in due parti, cioe in due semibrevi perfecte o loro valore. [11] Le corna ch'á'l lato dextro significano magior prolatione. [12] Ancora si segna con un meço cerchio sança alcuno punto, pure avendo le corna dal lato dextro. Exemplo: C· C

[13] La prolatione dello imperfecto minore á per suo segno un meço cerchio colle corna a mano sinistra con un punto, cosi: Ↄ [14] Uno punto a differentia del magior che n'á due. [15] Ancora si signa con un meço cerchio sança alcuno punto, a differentia del magiore imperfecto, colle corna da lato sinistro. Exemplo: Ↄ Ↄ

16: Titulus cognoscono le prolationi *ego*: -gnosce le -ne *cod.* 2 in *ego*: *forte* et *cod.*

COME S'ADOPERINO I DICTI SEGNI

[16] Sara uno imperfecto magior segnato col meço cerchio con punti, et infra il canto sara una certa parte d'imperfecto minore: si debba segnare quello imperfecto minore col meço cerchio co' punti. [17] Ma se il magiore é signato sança punto, el minore sara sança punto. [18] Et cosi si vuole intendere de' perfecti, pure che le corna de' meçi cerchi sianno inverso, come di sopra é dicto. Exemplo del dicto:

Ex. 39

(22v)

DELLA SINCOPA

17 *Sincopa* [1] La sincopa é uno rompere l'ordine della divisione in questo modo, con note seperate da quelle con chi si debbono acompagnare nella divisione del modo o del tempo, che dividendo o computando un canto, ti converra passare piu note o pose per riducerle con cui si debbono dividere et acompagnare. [2] In questo modo troverassi una maxima che di lungi ara le sue note che l'aranno a perficere, el per che ella sara imperfecta; et sara rossa o voita. [3] Fia el canto di modo perfecto conviensi serbare quella imperfecta et seguire l'altra

16 col *ego*: il *cod.*

secundo la divisione del modo; [4] et in fine t'avançeranno quelle che debbono perficere quella che s'é serbata. [5] Et allora quelle cotali computarle et metterle in quella imperfecta; et non pure della maxima ma d'ogni altra nota. Exemplo:

Ex. 40

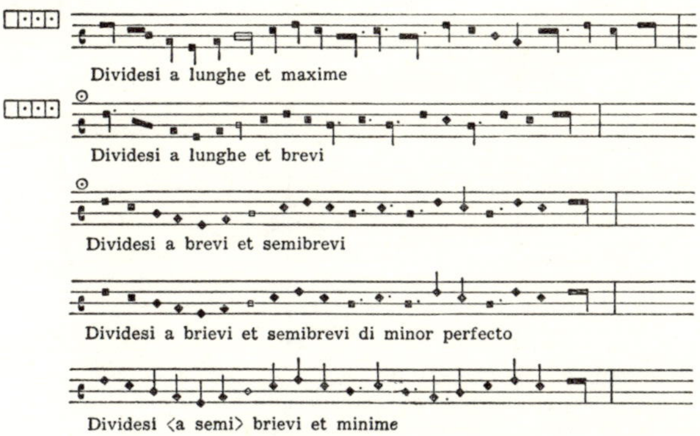

(23r)

DELLE POSE

[1] Avengha che delle pose dinança sia dicto, pure ne resta *18 Pose*
a dire alcuna cosa. [2] Et pero é da notare che, nelle sincope, posa di semibreve non puo essere sincopata dalla minima nelle magiori prolationi, né posa di brievi puo essere sincopata da semibreve in alcuna prolatione, posto che alcuni tenghino el contrario; ma Gian de Muris cosi ci amaestra [a].

DELLA DIMINUTIONE (23v)

[1] Per che intorno a cio é da notare che della maxima sara *19 Diminutione*
sua diminutione la longha; della longha, la breve; della breve,

[a] *LCM*, 7*b*, 7; publ. *CS*, 3, 57.

Exemplum 40d minime *ego*: -mi *cod.*

la semibreve; della semibreve, la minima; della minima, la semiminima; et quello medesmo si vuole intendere delle pose. [2] Ancora é da notare che quando un canto é di modo perfecto <et> di tempo imperfecto, la longha che varra tre brevi, a diminutione varra tre semibrevi. [3] Ma quando un canto sara di modo perfecto et tempo perfecto, la sua diminutione sara per terço. [4] Exemplo seguita del modo perfecto di tempo perfecto:

Ex. 41

<Tenor ANTE THRONUM TRINITATIS>

20 *Segni de' modi* [1] Restossi a dire dinançi alcuna cosa de' modi. [2] Et per tanto, i segni de' modi secundo Gian de Muris sono solamente due [a]. [3] Quello del modo perfecto é uno quadrangulo perfecto cum tre linee dentro et non áltro. [4] Ma quando si pone, é bisogna ancora porre el segno della prolatione: 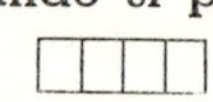 [5] E' el segno del modo imperfecto uno quadrangulo cum due vergole dentro: 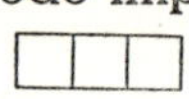 [6] Servono questi quadranguli a ogni prolatione; ma, come é dicto, bisogna porre **(24r)** il segno della prolatione. Et di cio basta.

CHE SIA COLORE O TAGLIA

21 *Colore o taglia* [1] Onde colore nella musicha pratica sara un processo di piu note con sincope <et> con spirationi, et poi, ripreso un'

[a] *LCM*, *4a*, 2; publ. *CS*, 3, 54.

20: 2 solamente *ego*: -ti *cod.* 5 *fig. posita post quadranguli seq. phrasis, in marg. cod.*

Exemplum 41b: 2 *1a pa. br.*, *2a pa. sb.*, *10-12 om.*, *15 B in cod.*

altra volta o piu, le medesime sincope et spirationi et valore, dissimili le voci. [2] Niente di meno taglia ancora é medessimo modo. [3] Ma usasi ne' tenori artificiali*, partendo il tinore in certe parti, si come el tinore di certi motetti, cioe LUCE CLARUS o SUB ARTURO o OMNI HABENTI.
Exemplo:

Ex. 42a 

Tenor LUCE CLARUS a tre taglie di valore a questo modo; ma in voce sono differentiate.

Ex. 42b 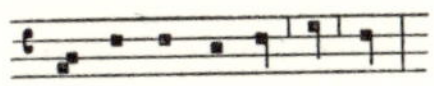

SUB ARTURO a tre taglie di valore; ma in voce sono differentiate.

Ex. 43 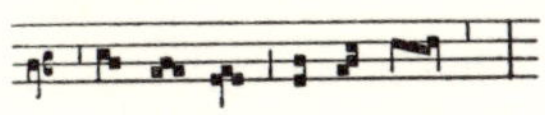

Tenor OMNI HABENTI a due taglie, non in medesma voce. [4] Pero che se fossono le taglie in valore et in medesima, voce, una compositione di note piu volte repetuta parebbe, et non altro.

DEO GRATIAS

21: 3 artificiali *ego*: artifici atificiati *cod.* sub Arturo *ego*: sabarturus *cod.*

Exemplum 42 *due partes super una scala continua cod.*

TABLE OF CHAPTERS

ANLYTICAL INDEX